HOT DIGGITY DOG

65 Great Recipes
Using Brats, Hot Dogs,
and Sausages

HOT DIGGITY DOG

ELIZA CROSS

PHOTOGRAPHS BY SHEENA BATES

GIBBS SMITH
TO ENRICH AND INSPIRE HUMANKIND

FOR FRANK

First Edition
26 25 24 23 22   5 4 3 2 1

Text © 2022 Eliza Cross
Photographs © 2022 Sheena Bates

Published by
Gibbs Smith
P.O. Box 667
Layton, Utah 84041

1.800.835.4993 orders
www.gibbs-smith.com

Designed by Dawn DeVries Sokol
Printed and bound in China

Gibbs Smith books are printed on either recycled, 100% post-consumer waste,
FSC-certified papers or on paper produced from sustainable PEFC-certified
forest/controlled wood source. Learn more at www.pefc.org.

Library of Congress Control Number: 2020942766
ISBN: 978-1-4236-5698-2

CONTENTS

INTRODUCTION

■ ■ ■ ■ ■ ■ ■ ■ ■ ■ ■ ■ ■ ■ ■ ■ ■ ■ ■

Have you ever noticed how brats, hot dogs, and sausages are often paired with memorable moments? Maybe you remember that perfect first snappy bite of a Chicago-style dog at your favorite ballpark, or the backyard bliss of a juicy bratwurst cooked on the grill for an alfresco summer dinner, or the cozy comfort of a hearty winter meal like smoked Polish sausage cooked with creamy, cheesy mashed potatoes.

Every country seems to have its own take on sausage, from British bangers to Portuguese linguiça to Spanish chorizo to German wurst. One of the oldest prepared foods in recorded history, the sausage was originally created as a way to preserve meats for longer storage before refrigeration was available. Lesser cuts and scraps were ground and combined with spices and a heavy dose of salt for curing; in fact, the word *sausage* derives from the Latin word *salsus*, which means "to prepare by salting."

These days, the humble sausage has been elevated to new culinary heights. In addition to traditional pork and beef varieties, artisanal sausages are crafted with everything from top-quality lamb, chicken, duck, game meats, and bison to vegan ingredients like mushrooms, chickpeas, and vital wheat gluten. Some links are even made from exotic meats like pricey Kobe beef, alligator, or rattlesnake.

This collection of easy-to-make recipes features sixty-five flavorful new ways to enjoy your favorite sausages and frankfurters. Try Beer-Glazed and Bacon-Wrapped Cheddar-Stuffed Brats (page 106). Enjoy Naan Dogs with Pineapple-Jalapeño Relish and Curried Honey Mustard (page 56). Hunker down with a generous bowl of High-on-the-Hog Jambalaya (page 113) or Grilled Romaine and Sausage Caesar Salad (page 87).

Feel free to improvise with your favorite sausages—exotic or otherwise—and make these recipes your own. I hope you'll enjoy some new memory-making moments while savoring the incomparable flavors of bratwurst, franks, and sausages. Hot diggity dog!

—Eliza Cross

HELPFUL HINTS

A Sausage for Every Appetite

The recipes in this book were developed using brats, hot dogs, and sausages commonly available at grocery stores, but feel free to experiment with your favorite links.

Hot dogs, frankfurters, and wieners are commonly made from finely ground beef, pork, chicken, turkey, or a blend of several meats plus spices and binders. After being formed and cooked, they may also be smoked for added flavor.

Link sausages and bratwurst are made from ground meats and spices and are typically formed in a natural casing. Artisan sausages often contain flavor-enhancing ingredients like cheese, onions, apples, peppers, berries, wine, brandy, and more.

Plant-based sausages and dogs provide tasty vegan and vegetarian alternatives to meat and are often enhanced with a fat like coconut oil to mimic the mouthfeel of traditional links.

Cooked to Perfection

Fresh meat-based sausages in casings should always be fully cooked to an internal temperature of 165 degrees F.

Precooked and smoked sausages need only be heated to an internal temperature of 160 degrees F since they have already been fully cooked during processing. They may be finished on a hot grill for a minute or two to add smoky flavor and grill marks.

For even cooking, allow plant-based sausages to come to room temperature before cooking. Follow package directions, as plant-based sausages generally need less cooking time than their meaty counterparts.

Grill Like a Pro

Whether you're using a charcoal or gas grill, lightly brush the grill grates with a high-smoke-point oil like peanut or grapeseed oil prior to cooking. Your brats, dogs, and sausages will be less likely to stick, making them easier to turn.

For even cooking (and great grill marks), arrange the links perpendicular to the grill grates.

Grill link sausages slowly over medium-low heat (between 300 and 350 degrees F) for the best results. Turn often so each side gets golden brown. Cook until the internal temperature reaches 165 degrees F.

Take care not to poke holes in juicy brats and sausages during cooking or the skins may split and the juices will leak out.

A Note about Casings

Some sausages have a casing that encapsulates the meat, and others do not. In most cases, the casing is natural and meant to be eaten. A casing of inedible material like cellulose or collagen is occasionally used in the production of specialty sausages and should be removed before eating.

Most hot dogs are skinless, but some have natural skins or casings. These franks typically stay juicier after cooking, and you'll notice the trademark "snap" when biting into the dog.

Link sausage can generally be substituted pound-for-pound when a recipe calls for bulk sausage; simply remove the ground meat from the casings before cooking.

BREAKFASTS AND BRUNCH

YORKSHIRE MAPLE SAUSAGE PANCAKE

3 large eggs

1/2 cup whole milk

1/2 teaspoon salt

1/2 cup all-purpose flour

1 pound maple pork breakfast sausage links

3 tablespoons butter, divided

1 tablespoon vegetable oil

Powdered sugar, for sprinkling

1/4 cup maple syrup, warmed

Preheat oven to 400 degrees F.

In a small bowl, whisk together eggs, milk, and salt. Add flour and whisk until blended. Allow batter to rest for 15 minutes. Meanwhile, cook sausage links in a large skillet over medium heat, turning occasionally, until browned and cooked through, 8–10 minutes. Drain on paper towels, then cut each sausage into 3 pieces.

Put 1 tablespoon of the butter and the oil in a 12-inch cast iron skillet and heat in the oven until butter melts, 3–4 minutes. Remove from oven and swirl to combine butter and oil. Stir the batter and pour into the warm skillet. Arrange the cooked sausage pieces evenly over the top. Return to the oven and bake until golden brown and puffed, 20–25 minutes. When the pancake is nearly done, melt remaining butter in a small saucepan over medium heat and keep warm.

Remove the skillet from the oven and sprinkle the pancake with powdered sugar. Cut into wedges, drizzle with melted butter and warm maple syrup, and serve.

KIELBASA AND HASH BROWN BAKE

MAKES 6 SERVINGS

2 teaspoons extra virgin olive oil

8 ounces kielbasa sausage,
   cut in 1/3-inch pieces

3 cups frozen shredded hash brown
   potatoes, thawed

3 tablespoons unsalted butter, melted

1/2 teaspoon salt

1/4 teaspoon freshly ground black pepper

6 large eggs, lightly beaten

2 cups shredded cheddar cheese

2 tablespoons finely chopped green onions

Preheat oven to 425 degrees F. Lightly grease a 9-inch deep-dish pie plate or ovenproof skillet.

In a large skillet, heat oil over medium-high heat until it shimmers. Add kielbasa and cook, stirring occasionally, until lightly browned. Drain on paper towels and set aside.

In a medium bowl, combine hash browns, butter, salt, and pepper and toss to combine. Press into the bottom and up the sides of the prepared pie plate. Bake until golden brown around the edges, about 25 minutes. Remove from oven and reduce oven temperature to 350 degrees F.

Pour the eggs evenly over the crust, arrange the kielbasa pieces evenly over the top, and sprinkle with cheese. Return to the oven and bake until eggs are set and top is lightly browned, about 30 minutes. Cool for 10 minutes, then sprinkle with green onions, cut into wedges, and serve.

SAUSAGE, GREEN CHILE, AND CHEESE STRATA

MAKES 8 SERVINGS

1 pound spicy or regular bulk pork sausage

1 small onion, chopped

6 English muffins, cut in 1/2-inch pieces

2 cups shredded sharp cheddar
   cheese, divided

1 1/2 cups shredded pepper jack
   cheese, divided

8 large eggs

1 1/2 cups sour cream

1/2 teaspoon salt

1/4 teaspoon freshly ground black pepper

1 (4-ounce) can chopped green
   chiles, drained

Chopped fresh chives, for garnish

In a large skillet, cook sausage over medium-high heat, breaking up the meat with a spatula, until cooked through and lightly browned. Drain on paper towels, finely crumble, and set aside.

Drain any excess grease from the skillet, add onion, and cook over medium-high heat until tender and just starting to brown, 6–8 minutes. Remove from heat and set aside.

Lightly grease a 9 x 13-inch baking pan and arrange English muffin pieces evenly in the pan. Top with half the sausage, half the onion, half the cheddar cheese, and half the pepper jack cheese.

In a large bowl, whisk eggs, sour cream, salt, pepper, and green chiles and pour evenly over sausage and cheese in baking pan. Scatter remaining sausage, onion, and cheeses on top. Cover and refrigerate for 8 hours or overnight to allow flavors to meld.

Preheat oven to 350 degrees F. Bake strata until lightly browned and set in the middle, 45–50 minutes. Let stand for 10 minutes, then sprinkle with chives, slice, and serve.

PUFF PASTRY CUPS WITH SAGE SAUSAGE, LEEKS, AND MUSHROOMS

MAKES 6 SERVINGS

6 frozen puff pastry shells (10-ounce package)

8 ounces sage or breakfast bulk pork sausage

2 tablespoons extra virgin olive oil

2 large leeks, white and pale green parts only, cleaned and thinly sliced

8 ounces button mushrooms, cut in 1/2-inch slices

2 cloves garlic, minced

1 cup heavy whipping cream

1/2 cup chicken stock

1/2 teaspoon salt

1/4 teaspoon freshly ground black pepper

Fresh flat-leaf parsley sprigs, for garnish

Grated Parmesan cheese, for garnish

Preheat oven to 400 degrees F. Line a baking sheet with parchment paper.

Arrange the frozen pastry shells on the prepared baking sheet and bake until puffed and golden brown, about 20 minutes. Cool on a wire rack for 5 minutes, then use a small paring knife to cut and lift out the center of each pastry shell. Set aside shells and centers.

In a large skillet, cook sausage over medium-high heat, breaking up the meat with a spatula, until cooked through and lightly browned. Drain on paper towels, finely crumble, and set aside.

(continued)

Wipe out the skillet, add the oil, and heat over medium-high until oil shimmers. Add the leeks and cook until tender, about 3 minutes. Add the mushrooms and garlic and cook, stirring frequently, until mushrooms are lightly browned, about 8 minutes. Add the cooked sausage, cream, stock, salt, and pepper and continue cooking, stirring frequently, until mixture reduces slightly and thickens, about 6 minutes. Remove from heat and cool for 5 minutes.

Arrange the puff pastry shells on individual plates and spoon the sausage mixture into the shells. Garnish with parsley and Parmesan cheese, angle the pastry centers on top, and serve.

SAUSAGE AND SPINACH QUICHE

MAKES 6 SERVINGS

2 teaspoons extra virgin olive oil

8 ounces fully cooked chicken or pork sausage links, cut in 1/3-inch slices

1 small onion, chopped

4 ounces button mushrooms, cut in 1/4-inch slices

4 ounces baby spinach

1 unbaked 9-inch pie shell

6 large eggs

1 cup milk

1/2 teaspoon salt

1/4 teaspoon freshly ground black pepper

1 1/2 tablespoons shredded Parmesan cheese

Preheat oven to 350 degrees F.

In a large skillet, heat the oil over medium-high heat until it shimmers. Add sausage slices and cook, stirring occasionally, until lightly browned. Drain on paper towels and set aside.

Return the skillet to the stove, add onion, and cook over medium-high heat until softened and translucent, 5–6 minutes. Add mushrooms and cook for 2–3 minutes. Add spinach and cook until liquid evaporates and spinach is wilted, about 4 minutes. Add browned sausage, stir, and remove from heat. Spoon the mixture evenly into the pie shell.

In a medium bowl, whisk together the eggs, milk, salt, and pepper, then pour evenly over the sausage mixture. Sprinkle with Parmesan cheese. Bake the quiche until the eggs are set and a knife inserted in the center comes out clean, about 40 minutes. Allow to cool for 10 minutes, then slice and serve.

SAUSAGE FRENCH TOAST CRISPIES

MAKES 6 SERVINGS

½ cup packed dark brown sugar

½ teaspoon ground cinnamon

12 pork breakfast sausage links

12 slices white or whole-wheat
  sandwich bread

3 large eggs

1 tablespoon milk

½ teaspoon vanilla extract

1 tablespoon butter

Powdered sugar, for sprinkling

Maple syrup, warmed, for drizzling

Preheat oven to 375 degrees F. Line a baking sheet with parchment paper.

In a shallow bowl, combine the brown sugar and cinnamon and set aside.

In a large skillet, cook sausage links over medium-high heat, turning frequently, until cooked through and lightly browned. Drain on paper towels.

Roll each slice of bread flat with a rolling pin and trim off the crusts. Place 1 cooked sausage link at the edge of each bread slice and roll up, pressing gently to seal.

In a bowl, whisk together the eggs, milk, and vanilla. Heat the butter in a large skillet over medium-high heat until it begins to foam. Dip each bread roll in the egg mixture, shaking off excess. Cook the rolls in batches in the skillet, turning frequently, until all sides are golden brown. Remove with tongs and immediately roll in the brown sugar–cinnamon mixture, turning to coat. Transfer rolls to the prepared baking sheet and bake until hot and crispy, about 6 minutes. Cool for 5 minutes, sprinkle with powdered sugar, and serve with warm maple syrup.

BREAKFAST DOGS

MAKES 6 SERVINGS

6 1/2 tablespoons unsalted butter, softened, divided

1/3 cup all-purpose flour

3 cups whole milk, warmed

1/2 teaspoon salt, plus more for seasoning

1/4 teaspoon freshly ground black pepper, plus more for seasoning

1 cup shredded sharp cheddar cheese

1/4 cup shredded Parmesan cheese

6 hot dog buns, split

6 jumbo all-beef hot dogs

6 large eggs

1/3 cup half-and-half

6 strips bacon, cooked until crisp and then crumbled

Chopped fresh chives, for garnish

In a medium saucepan, melt 4 tablespoons of the butter over medium-high heat. Add the flour and cook, stirring constantly, until the mixture is pale yellow and frothy, about 1 minute. Slowly add the warm milk and continue whisking until sauce thickens and bubbles, 3–4 minutes. Reduce heat to a simmer, season with the salt and pepper, and simmer for 2 minutes. Add the cheeses and whisk until melted. Cover and keep warm over very low heat.

(continued)

Open the buns and spread cut sides with 2 tablespoons of the butter. Heat a large skillet over medium-high heat and cook the buns, buttered side down, until golden brown, working in batches if necessary. Set aside.

With a sharp knife, cut the hot dogs lengthwise to within 1/4 inch without cutting all the way through. Gently open the hot dogs and arrange on the hot skillet, cut side down. Press down with a spatula and cook until browned and heated through, about 6 minutes, then set aside.

In a medium bowl, whisk together eggs and half-and-half. Wipe out the skillet and melt remaining butter over medium heat. Add egg mixture and cook, stirring frequently, until eggs are scrambled. Remove from heat and season with salt and pepper to taste.

To assemble, place an open-face grilled bun on each plate. Top with a hot dog, open side up, followed by a portion of scrambled eggs. Spoon the sauce over the eggs, sprinkle with crumbled bacon and chives, and serve.

BRATWURST, POTATO, AND SWISS SKILLET

MAKES 4 TO 6 SERVINGS

1 tablespoon butter

2 fully cooked bratwurst links,
 cut in 1/3-inch slices

1/2 cup chopped onion

1 pound russet potatoes, peeled and
 cut in 1/2-inch dice

1/2 teaspoon salt, plus more for seasoning

1/8 teaspoon freshly ground black pepper,
 plus more for seasoning

2 ounces Swiss cheese, shredded

6 large eggs

1/2 cup milk

Chopped fresh flat-leaf parsley, for garnish

In a large skillet, melt the butter over medium-high heat until it foams. Add the bratwurst slices and cook, stirring occasionally, until lightly browned. Drain on paper towels and set aside.

Add the onion to the skillet, reduce heat to medium, and cook until translucent and tender, about 5 minutes. With a slotted spoon, transfer to a small bowl and set aside. Add the potatoes to the skillet, sprinkle with salt and pepper, stir, and then spread in a single layer. Cover skillet and cook, checking occasionally, until the potatoes are lightly browned, 7–9 minutes. Flip the potatoes and continue cooking, uncovered, until browned and tender, 6–8 more minutes.

Scatter the browned bratwurst, onion, and cheese evenly over the potatoes. In a medium bowl, whisk together the eggs and milk, then pour evenly over the mixture in the skillet. Cook over medium heat, covered, until cheese is melted and eggs are set, about 10 minutes. Season with salt and pepper to taste, garnish with parsley, cut into wedges, and serve.

VANILLA-BUTTERMILK PANCAKE SAUSAGE SLIDERS

MAKES 6 SLIDERS

1 pound regular or maple bulk pork breakfast sausage

2 cups all-purpose flour

2 teaspoons baking powder

1 teaspoon baking soda

1/2 teaspoon salt

2 cups buttermilk

6 tablespoons unsalted butter, melted

2 large eggs

2 teaspoons vanilla extract

Maple syrup, warmed, for drizzling

Form the sausage into 6 equal-size patties, about 3 1/2 inches in diameter. Heat a large skillet over medium-high heat and cook the sausage patties, pressing down with a spatula occasionally, until golden brown. Flip and continue cooking until cooked through and well browned on both sides, about 10 minutes total. Drain on paper towels and set aside.

In a mixing bowl, whisk together the flour, baking powder, baking soda, and salt until well blended. Make a well in the center and add the buttermilk, butter, eggs, and vanilla. Mix just until blended. (For tender pancakes, do not overmix.)

(continued)

Wipe out the skillet, spray with nonstick cooking spray, and heat over medium heat. Working in batches, pour batter in generous 2-tablespoon portions to create pancakes that are about 3 inches in diameter. Cook until bubbles start to form on the top and the bottom is golden brown. Flip and cook until the other side is golden brown. Keep warm while cooking remaining pancakes. You will need 12 pancakes.

To serve, place 1 pancake on a plate, drizzle with a little maple syrup, add a sausage patty, and top with another pancake.

APPETIZERS

MINI CORN DOG BITES

MAKES 18 PIECES
■ ■ ■ ■ ■ ■ ■

1 cup cornmeal

1 cup plus 2 tablespoons all-purpose
  flour, divided

1/4 cup sugar

4 teaspoons baking powder

1/4 teaspoon salt

1/8 teaspoon freshly ground black pepper

1 large egg

1 cup milk

3/4 cup ketchup

2 tablespoons yellow mustard

1 quart peanut oil, for frying

6 all-beef hot dogs

In a medium mixing bowl, whisk together cornmeal, 1 cup flour, sugar, baking powder, salt, and pepper. Add the egg and milk and stir just until batter is smooth. Refrigerate batter for 30 minutes.

In a small bowl, whisk together ketchup and mustard; set aside.

Pour oil into a deep fryer or heavy-bottom saucepan and heat to 350 degrees F.

Remove batter from refrigerator. Pat the hot dogs dry with paper towels, cut in thirds, and put them in a medium bowl. Sprinkle with remaining flour, tossing to coat. Spear each hot dog piece with a fork and dunk in batter, coating completely. Using another fork, gently slide the batter-coated hot dogs into the hot oil, cooking several at a time. Cook until golden brown, then turn over with a fork and continue cooking until other side is golden brown, about 3 minutes total. Drain on paper towels. Arrange on a platter and serve with sauce.

BRUSCHETTA WITH SAUSAGE, SAGE, AND FONTINA

MAKES 24 PIECES

6 to 8 ounces mild Italian sausage
(links or bulk)
1 long French baguette,
cut in 1/2-inch-thick slices
Extra virgin olive oil, for brushing
1 1/2 cups shredded fontina cheese

1 tablespoon finely chopped fresh sage
1/4 teaspoon freshly ground black pepper
2 Roma tomatoes, finely chopped
and drained
Chopped fresh chives, for garnish

Preheat oven broiler. Line a baking sheet with aluminum foil.

If using sausage links, remove casings. Crumble sausage into a medium skillet and cook over medium heat, breaking up the meat with a spatula, until lightly browned, 7–8 minutes. Drain and set aside.

Meanwhile, arrange the bread slices on the prepared baking sheet and brown lightly on both sides under the broiler. Remove from oven and brush bread with oil; set aside. Turn off broiler and heat oven to 400 degrees F.

In a medium bowl, combine the cheese, cooked sausage, sage, and pepper. Spread the mixture evenly over the toasted bread slices and bake until cheese melts, about 5 minutes. Remove from oven and cool for 5 minutes. Sprinkle with tomatoes and chives and serve.

KIELBASA WITH BEER-CHEESE FONDUE

MAKES 6 SERVINGS

2 teaspoons vegetable oil

1 pound kielbasa sausage, cut on the
diagonal in 1/4-inch slices

2 tablespoons all-purpose flour

1/2 teaspoon salt

1/4 teaspoon freshly ground black pepper

2 cups shredded sharp cheddar cheese

2 cups shredded Swiss cheese

1 clove garlic, halved

1 (12-ounce) bottle or can regular or
nonalcoholic beer

3 drops hot pepper sauce

Heat the oil in a large skillet over medium-high heat. Add kielbasa and cook, turning once, until browned and sizzling. Drain on paper towels and set aside.

In a medium bowl, combine flour, salt, and pepper. Add the cheddar and Swiss cheeses and toss with a fork to coat with the flour mixture. Rub the garlic halves around the bottom and sides of a fondue pot or a heavy-bottom saucepan.

Pour beer into fondue pot and slowly bring to a simmer over medium-low heat, about 5 minutes. Gradually add cheese mixture, a handful at a time, stirring after each addition until cheese is melted and smooth. Add hot pepper sauce and stir until smooth. Skewer the browned kielbasa slices with cocktail toothpicks and serve with the warm fondue for dunking.

GERMAN POTATO SKINS

MAKES 12 PIECES

6 medium russet potatoes, well scrubbed

3 tablespoons unsalted butter, melted

1/4 teaspoon salt

1/4 teaspoon freshly ground black pepper

1 (12-ounce) bottle or can regular or
   nonalcoholic beer

3 (4-ounce) fresh bratwurst or German
   sausage links

1 1/2 cups shredded Swiss cheese

1/3 cup grated Parmesan cheese

Chopped fresh chives, for garnish

Preheat oven to 400 degrees F. Line a baking sheet with aluminum foil.

Prick the potatoes in several places with a fork. Bake directly on center oven rack until fork-tender, about 1 hour. Set aside until cool enough to handle. Increase oven temperature to 450 degrees F. Cut potatoes in half lengthwise. Using a small spoon or melon baller, scoop out the potato flesh, leaving a 1/4-inch-thick shell (reserve the potato flesh for another use). Arrange the shells, cut side up, on prepared baking sheet. Brush potato shells inside and out with butter and season with salt and pepper. Bake until lightly browned, about 10 minutes, then cool on baking sheet.

Pour beer into a medium skillet and add bratwurst. Bring to a boil over medium-high heat. Reduce heat to medium-low, cover, and simmer for 10 minutes. Remove bratwurst, pour out beer, and dry the pan. Return bratwurst to pan and cook over medium heat, turning often, until browned all over, about 6 minutes. Drain on paper towels and thinly slice.

Preheat oven broiler. Sprinkle 1 tablespoon Swiss cheese in bottom of each potato shell. Divide sliced bratwurst among the shells and top each with another 1 tablespoon Swiss cheese. Sprinkle with Parmesan cheese. Broil until cheese melts and starts to brown, 1–2 minutes. Cool for 5 minutes, then sprinkle with chopped chives and serve.

SAUSAGE SKEWERS WITH HOISIN DIPPING SAUCE

MAKES 6 TO 8 SERVINGS

For the sauce

1/3 cup hoisin sauce

1/3 cup firmly packed dark brown sugar

2 tablespoons rice vinegar

2 tablespoons Sichuan chili paste

1 tablespoon tamari or soy sauce

1 tablespoon honey

2 cloves garlic, finely minced

1 teaspoon minced fresh ginger

For the skewers

1 pound smoked sausage links,
   cut in 1/2-inch slices

2 cups fresh or canned pineapple
   chunks, drained

Sesame seeds, for garnish

Preheat oven to 375 degrees F. Line a baking sheet with parchment paper.

To make the sauce, whisk together the hoisin sauce, brown sugar, rice vinegar, chili paste, tamari, honey, garlic, and ginger in a small saucepan. Cook over medium-high heat, stirring frequently, until mixture just starts to boil. Reduce heat to medium-low and simmer for 3 minutes. Remove pan from heat and set aside.

Arrange sausage slices in a single layer on prepared baking sheet and top each with a pineapple chunk. Brush generously with sauce and bake until lightly browned, about 10 minutes. Remove from oven, brush again with sauce, and continue baking until browned and sizzling, 6–7 minutes. Remove from oven and cool for 5 minutes.

Thread several sausage slices and pineapple chunks on a skewer. Arrange skewers on a serving platter, sprinkle with sesame seeds, and serve with the remaining sauce for dipping.

CHORIZO QUESO DIP

MAKES 6 PIECES

8 ounces mild Colby cheese, shredded
8 ounces Monterey Jack cheese, shredded
1 tablespoon all-purpose flour
6 ounces bulk chorizo sausage
2 green onions, finely chopped

1 jalapeño pepper, seeded and finely
   chopped (or substitute 1 Anaheim chile
   for less heat)
1/8 teaspoon salt
3/4 cup regular or nonalcoholic lager beer
1/4 cup fresh pico de gallo or salsa
Yellow and blue tortilla chips, for serving

In a large bowl, combine cheeses and flour and toss until evenly coated; set aside.

Crumble chorizo into a medium saucepan and cook over medium heat until crispy, 8–10 minutes.
Drain on paper towels, finely crumble, and set aside.

Pour out all but about 1 teaspoon drippings and return saucepan to medium heat. Add green
onions, jalapeño, and salt and cook until tender, 2–3 minutes. Whisk in beer and bring to a simmer,
stirring occasionally. Gradually add cheese mixture, a handful at a time, stirring after each addition,
until cheese is melted and smooth. Stir in half the crumbled chorizo. Transfer mixture to a serving
dish. Top with remaining chorizo and a swirl of pico de gallo. Serve with tortilla chips.

KIELBASA-JALAPEÑO POPPERS

MAKES 24 PIECES

1 tablespoon butter

8 ounces kielbasa sausage, chopped in
 ¼-inch pieces

8 ounces cream cheese, softened

½ cup grated Parmesan cheese

½ cup shredded cheddar cheese

½ teaspoon onion powder

¼ teaspoon salt

¼ teaspoon freshly ground black pepper

12 large jalapeño peppers, halved
 lengthwise and seeded

Preheat oven to 425 degrees F. Lightly grease a baking sheet.

In a medium skillet, melt the butter over medium heat. Add the kielbasa and cook, stirring occasionally, until lightly browned, 6–7 minutes. Remove pan from heat and cool for 10 minutes.

Transfer the kielbasa to a medium bowl and add the cream cheese, Parmesan cheese, cheddar cheese, onion powder, salt, and pepper. Mix well. Spoon about 1 tablespoon of the mixture into each jalapeño half. Arrange the stuffed halves on prepared baking sheet. Bake until bubbly and lightly browned, about 20 minutes. Serve warm.

SAUSAGE-STUFFED MUSHROOMS

MAKES 12 PIECES

12 large button mushrooms

2 tablespoons butter

2 tablespoons chopped sweet onion
  (such as Vidalia)

1 tablespoon fresh lemon juice

1 tablespoon chopped fresh basil

Salt and freshly ground black pepper

4 ounces bulk Italian sausage

1 tablespoon chopped fresh flat-leaf parsley

2 tablespoons dry breadcrumbs

2 tablespoons grated Parmesan cheese

Chopped fresh chives, for garnish

Preheat oven to 400 degrees F. Lightly grease a baking sheet.

Remove stems from mushrooms and finely chop. Arrange mushroom caps, stemmed side up, on prepared baking sheet.

In a medium skillet, melt butter over medium-high heat. Add onion and mushroom stems and cook until tender, about 5 minutes. Add lemon juice and basil, season with salt and pepper to taste, and cook until most of the liquid has evaporated. Transfer onion mixture to a medium bowl and cool slightly.

Add sausage and parsley to onion mixture and mix until well combined. Divide mixture evenly among mushroom caps, mounding slightly to fill. Stir together breadcrumbs and Parmesan cheese and sprinkle mixture over the filling in the mushroom caps.

Bake stuffed mushrooms until tops start to brown and sausage is cooked through, about 20 minutes. Cool on baking sheet for 5 minutes, then sprinkle with chopped chives and serve.

ITALIAN SAUSAGE PARTY SUB

MAKES 12 PIECES

1 tablespoon extra virgin olive oil

4 (3- to 4-ounce) Italian sausage links

1 long Italian bread loaf, halved lengthwise

1/2 cup marinara sauce

4 small Roma tomatoes, thinly sliced

1/4 cup chopped fresh basil leaves

1 small green bell pepper, seeded and sliced

1/2 small red onion, sliced (optional)

Salt and freshly ground black pepper

6 ounces provolone cheese, sliced

Preheat oven to 350 degrees F.

In a large skillet, heat oil over medium heat. Add the sausages and cook, turning occasionally, until cooked through and browned, 10–12 minutes. Drain on paper towels, then cut on the diagonal in 1/4-inch slices.

Spread the bottom half of the bread with marinara sauce and layer with browned sausage. Top with tomatoes, basil, bell pepper, and onion (if using) and season with salt and pepper to taste. Top with the provolone slices. Place the upper half of the bread on top and wrap the sandwich in aluminum foil.

Bake until the sandwich is hot and the cheese is fully melted, 15–20 minutes. Cool slightly. Unwrap the sandwich and cut into 12 pieces. Arrange on a platter and serve.

NEW ORLEANS ANDOUILLE-SHRIMP SKEWERS

MAKES ABOUT 40 PIECES

For the remoulade sauce

1 cup mayonnaise

¼ cup chili sauce

2 tablespoons Creole mustard

2 tablespoons extra virgin olive oil

2 tablespoons fresh lemon juice

2 teaspoons hot sauce

1 teaspoon Worcestershire sauce

½ teaspoon chili powder

1 teaspoon salt

½ teaspoon freshly ground black pepper

¼ teaspoon garlic powder

4 medium green onions, finely chopped

2 tablespoons chopped fresh
 flat-leaf parsley

2 tablespoons minced celery

2 teaspoons capers, lightly chopped

For the skewers

2 tablespoons extra virgin olive oil

3 tablespoons Cajun seasoning

1½ pounds large shrimp, peeled
 and deveined

12 ounces smoked andouille sausage links

1 tablespoon chopped fresh flat-leaf parsley

To make the remoulade sauce, whisk together mayonnaise, chili sauce, mustard, oil, lemon juice, hot sauce, Worcestershire sauce, chili powder, salt, pepper, and garlic powder in a medium bowl until smooth. Add green onions, parsley, celery, and capers and stir to blend. Cover and refrigerate.

To make the skewers, whisk together oil and Cajun seasoning in a large bowl. Add shrimp and stir to coat. Cover and refrigerate, turning occasionally, for 1 hour.

Preheat a grill to medium-high. Cut sausage in even slices, spacing cuts so you will have 1 sausage slice for each shrimp. Thread 1 shrimp and 1 sausage slice on each skewer or toothpick. Spray a grill basket with nonstick spray and heat on the grill for 2 minutes. Add skewers in a single layer and grill, turning once, until shrimp are opaque and sausage is hot, about 3 minutes per side. Arrange skewers on a platter, sprinkle with parsley, and serve with remoulade sauce.

SPICY SAUSAGE RANGOONS WITH AVOCADO RANCH SAUCE

MAKES 24 PIECES

For the sauce
1 ripe avocado, peeled and pitted
1/2 cup ranch salad dressing
Salt and freshly ground black pepper

For the rangoons
6 ounces spicy Italian sausage
  (links or bulk)

1 medium jalapeño, seeded and finely diced
2 green onions, finely chopped
1/2 cup finely shredded pepper jack cheese
1 large egg white
1 teaspoon water
24 (3 1/2-inch) square wonton wrappers
2 cups peanut oil

To make the sauce, mash the avocado with a fork in a small bowl. Add the ranch dressing, season with salt and pepper to taste, and stir until well blended. Cover and refrigerate.

To make the rangoons, if using sausage links, remove the casings. Crumble the sausage into a medium skillet and cook over medium heat, breaking up the meat with a spatula, until cooked through and lightly browned, 7–8 minutes. Drain on paper towels, cool, and finely crumble.

Transfer the sausage to a small bowl and add the jalapeño, green onions, and cheese. Mix well.

In a small bowl, whisk together egg white and water. Lay 1 wonton wrapper on a flat surface and cover the rest with a damp paper towel to keep them moist. Scoop a heaping teaspoon of sausage mixture into the center of the wrapper. Moisten edges of wrapper with the egg white mixture and bring the 4 corners together, pinching edges to seal. Repeat to use remaining filling and wrappers.

Pour oil into a deep fryer or heavy-bottom saucepan and heat to 350 degrees F. Working in batches, fry the rangoons until golden brown and crispy, gently turning with a slotted spoon or strainer to brown evenly, about 3 minutes total. Drain on paper towels and serve with the avocado ranch sauce.

ITALIAN SAUSAGE CAPRESE SKEWERS

MAKES 35 PIECES

1/2 cup balsamic vinegar

2 tablespoons honey

5 (4-ounce) Italian sausage links,
   each cut in 7 equal slices

1 bunch fresh basil

1 pound mini fresh mozzarella
   cheese balls, drained

1 pint small grape tomatoes

In a small saucepan, whisk together balsamic vinegar and honey and bring to a boil over medium-high heat. Reduce heat to low and simmer until mixture thickens slightly, about 4 minutes. Remove from heat and cool to room temperature.

Meanwhile, in a large skillet, cook sausage slices over medium heat, turning once, until cooked through and lightly browned, 8–10 minutes. Drain on paper towels and set aside.

For each skewer, thread 1 piece of sausage, 1 basil leaf, 1 mozzarella ball, and 1 tomato on a cocktail toothpick. Arrange skewers on a platter, drizzle with balsamic glaze, and serve.

SANDWICHES

GRILLED BRATWURST REUBEN PANINI

For the dressing

1/4 cup mayonnaise

1 tablespoon ketchup

1 tablespoon sweet pickle relish

1/8 teaspoon salt

1/8 teaspoon garlic powder

1/8 teaspoon onion powder

Dash hot pepper sauce

For the sandwiches

4 (3- to 4-ounce) fresh bratwurst links

4 soft hoagie rolls, split

8 slices Swiss cheese

1 cup prepared sauerkraut, well drained

2 tablespoons butter, softened

To make the dressing, whisk together the mayonnaise, ketchup, pickle relish, salt, garlic powder, onion powder, and pepper sauce in a small bowl until well blended. Cover and set aside.

To make the sandwiches, preheat a grill to medium. Grill brats, turning often, until browned and cooked through, 15–20 minutes. Transfer brats to a cutting board and cut on the diagonal in 1/2-inch slices.

Spread inside of the roll bottoms with half the dressing. Top each with 1 cheese slice. Top each cheese slice with 2 tablespoons sauerkraut. Divide bratwurst slices evenly among rolls and top each with 2 more tablespoons sauerkraut and another cheese slice. Spread inside of the roll tops with the remaining dressing and place on top of sandwiches. Spread outside of the roll tops with half the softened butter.

Heat a large skillet or panini griddle over medium heat. Arrange sandwiches in the pan, buttered top side down. Spread outside of the roll bottoms (now on top) with remaining butter and cook sandwiches until the cheese melts and bread is golden brown; flip and cook until the other side is golden brown. Remove from the pan, cut in half on the diagonal, and serve.

CHICKEN SAUSAGE, RED PEPPER, AND DILL HAVARTI SANDWICHES

MAKES 4 SERVINGS

1 tablespoon extra virgin olive oil

4 (3- to 4-ounce) chicken sausage links

8 slices sourdough bread

8 slices dill Havarti cheese

1 (12-ounce) jar roasted red bell peppers, drained

2 tablespoons butter, softened

Heat oil in a medium skillet over medium-high heat. Cook the sausages, turning occasionally, until browned and cooked through, 8–10 minutes. Drain on paper towels, then cut each link in half lengthwise and widthwise to make 4 pieces; set aside.

Top 4 bread slices each with 1 cheese slice. Cover cheese with roasted red pepper slices, cutting to fit. (Save any remaining peppers for another use.) Divide sausage pieces among sandwiches, then top with the remaining cheese and bread slices. Spread tops of the sandwiches with half the butter.

Heat a large skillet over medium heat and place sandwiches in the pan, buttered side down. Spread the tops with remaining butter and cook until cheese melts and bread is golden brown; flip and cook until the other side is golden brown. Remove from pan, cut in half, and serve.

CHILE RELLENO POPPER DOGS

MAKES 6 SERVINGS

6 Anaheim chiles (about 6 inches long)

6 all-beef hot dogs

1/3 cup shredded cheddar jack cheese

12 strips regular-cut bacon

6 flour tortillas, warmed

1/2 cup shredded lettuce

1 medium tomato, chopped

Salsa and sour cream, for serving

Preheat a grill to medium-high. Place chiles directly on the grill and cook, turning often, until skin blackens and blisters, 6–8 minutes. Put chiles in a paper bag, fold over the top, and let steam for 20 minutes. Reduce grill temperature to medium.

Peel skins from the chiles and wipe with a paper towel. Cut stems off and carefully make a lengthwise cut from the stem end to the tip without cutting all the way through. Spread open chiles and use a paring knife to remove the seeds and ribs from the interior.

Cut a slit down the length of each hot dog, being careful not to cut all the way through. Spoon 1 scant tablespoon of cheese inside each hot dog and stuff a hot dog inside each chile shell. Wrap each stuffed chile evenly with 2 bacon strips, securing with toothpicks.

Grill the stuffed chiles over indirect heat, turning often, until bacon is crispy and brown, about 8 minutes. Place each bacon-wrapped dog in a warm tortilla, sprinkle with lettuce and tomato, and serve with salsa and sour cream.

SMOKED BEEF DOG BBQ SANDWICHES

MAKES 6 SERVINGS

1/2 cup ketchup

2 tablespoons packed brown sugar

2 tablespoons Worcestershire sauce

1 tablespoon apple cider vinegar

1 teaspoon liquid smoke

Dash hot pepper sauce

1 teaspoon garlic powder

1/4 teaspoon ground mustard

1/4 teaspoon salt

1 pound all-beef jumbo hot dogs, cut on the diagonal in 1/4-inch slices

6 onion buns, split

6 slices medium cheddar cheese

12 dill pickle sandwich slices, drained

Preheat oven broiler.

In a small saucepan, stir together ketchup, brown sugar, Worcestershire sauce, vinegar, liquid smoke, hot pepper sauce, garlic powder, ground mustard, and salt. Bring to a simmer over medium heat and cook for 10 minutes. Remove from heat, cover, and set aside.

In a large skillet, cook the hot dog slices over medium heat, turning once, until browned, about 10 minutes. Add the sauce, stir, and heat until bubbling; set aside.

Arrange the buns, cut side up, on a baking sheet and broil, watching carefully, until lightly toasted, 1–2 minutes. Remove from oven and place a slice of cheese on each bottom bun. Spoon the hot dog mixture on top of cheese, top with pickle slices and top buns, and serve.

NAAN DOGS WITH PINEAPPLE-JALAPEÑO RELISH AND CURRIED HONEY MUSTARD

MAKES 4 SERVINGS

For the pineapple-jalapeño relish

2 tablespoons fresh lemon juice

1 tablespoon honey

1/4 teaspoon salt

1 1/2 cups finely diced fresh pineapple

1 large jalapeño, seeded and minced

1/2 cup finely diced English cucumber
  (seeds removed)

1/4 cup finely diced red bell pepper

For the curried honey mustard

1/2 cup mayonnaise

1/2 cup honey

1/4 cup Dijon mustard

1/2 teaspoon curry powder

For the hot dogs

6 fresh naan breads

6 jumbo all-beef hot dogs

Preheat oven to 300 degrees F.

To make the relish, whisk together lemon juice, honey, and salt in a small bowl. Add pineapple, jalapeño, cucumber, and bell pepper and stir to combine. Cover and refrigerate.

To make the curried honey mustard, combine mayonnaise, honey, mustard, and curry powder in a small bowl and stir until well blended. Cover and refrigerate.

To make the hot dogs, wrap naan in aluminum foil. Heat in the oven until warm, about 5 minutes.

Bring a large saucepan of water to a boil over high heat. Add hot dogs. Cover the pan, remove from heat, and let sit for 5 minutes. Remove the hot dogs with tongs and drain on paper towels.

Spread each warm naan bread with some of the honey mustard and top with a hot dog. Spoon some of the relish on top and serve.

CHILI DOGS
IN THE ROUND

MAKES 8 SERVINGS

For the chili sauce

8 ounces lean ground beef

8 ounces bulk spicy Italian sausage

1 small onion, chopped

1 clove garlic, minced

1 (15-ounce) can tomato sauce

1/4 cup beef stock

1 tablespoon chili powder

2 teaspoons ground cumin

1/2 teaspoon salt

1/2 teaspoon freshly ground black pepper

1/8 teaspoon cayenne pepper (optional)

For the sandwiches

8 bun-length skinless hot dogs

8 hamburger buns, split

1/2 cup shredded medium cheddar cheese

1/2 small red onion, thinly sliced (optional)

To make the chili sauce, cook ground beef, sausage, and onion in a large skillet over medium heat until meat is browned and onion is tender. Drain the excess grease, add garlic, and cook for 1 minute, stirring constantly. Add tomato sauce, stock, chili powder, cumin, salt, black pepper, and cayenne (if using) and stir well to combine. Cook for 30 minutes, stirring occasionally, until hot and bubbling. Cover and keep warm.

To make the sandwiches, preheat a grill to medium-high. Make 1/2-inch-deep cuts along 1 side of each hot dog at 1/2-inch intervals, being careful to not cut all the way through. Grill hot dogs until the cut sides begin to curl, about 3 minutes. Flip and continue cooking until the dogs are crispy and heated through, about 3 more minutes. Transfer to a platter and use your fingers to shape into circles. Arrange the hamburger buns on the grill, cut side down, and grill just until lightly toasted, 1–2 minutes.

Place a hot dog ring on each bottom bun. Fill the center with hot chili and top with cheese and red onion. Cover with the top buns, and serve.

CUBAN SANDWICHES FRANCISCO

MAKES 4 SERVINGS

4 jumbo all-beef hot dogs

1 large baguette, halved lengthwise

1/3 cup mayonnaise

8 slices Swiss cheese

8 dill pickle sandwich slices, drained

8 ounces sliced smoked ham

1/4 cup yellow mustard

3 tablespoons butter, melted and cooled

Preheat a grill to medium-high. Cook the hot dogs, turning often, until sizzling and browned all over, 6–8 minutes. Transfer to a cutting board and cut on the diagonal in 1/2-inch slices.

Spread the cut sides of bread halves with mayonnaise. Layer the bottom half with 4 cheese slices, cooked hot dog slices, pickles, and ham. Drizzle with mustard and top with the remaining cheese slices and top half of bread. Brush the outside top with half the butter, then cut in half crosswise to make 2 sandwiches.

Heat a large skillet or panini griddle over medium heat. Place sandwiches in the pan, buttered top side down. Brush the outside bottoms (now on top) with remaining butter and cook sandwiches, pressing down with a spatula if using a skillet, until cheese melts and bread is golden brown; flip and cook other side until golden brown. Remove from the pan, cut each half on the diagonal, and serve.

GRILLED BEER BRATS WITH BACON AND CARAMELIZED ONION RELISH

MAKES 8 SERVINGS

8 strips thick-cut bacon

2 large sweet yellow onions, halved and cut in 1/4-inch slices

2 cups regular or nonalcoholic beer

1 teaspoon salt

1/2 teaspoon freshly ground black pepper

8 fresh bratwurst links

8 hoagie or large hot dog buns, split

Stone-ground mustard, for serving

Cook bacon in a large skillet until brown and crispy. Reserve the drippings and drain bacon on paper towels; crumble and set aside. Add onions to the pan and cook over medium-low heat, stirring occasionally, until golden brown and caramelized, 30–40 minutes. Transfer onions to a large, heavy aluminum foil pan.

Preheat a grill to medium. Place the foil pan over indirect heat. Stir in the beer, salt, and pepper and cover pan with foil. Grill the brats over direct heat, turning often, until browned and cooked through, 15–20 minutes. Transfer brats to the onion mixture, cover again with foil, and simmer for at least 30 minutes and up to 2 hours.

Grill the buns, cut side down, until lightly toasted, 1–2 minutes. Add crumbled bacon to the onion mixture and stir until combined. To serve, place a bratwurst in each bun and use a slotted spoon to top each bratwurst with some of the onion relish. Serve with stone-ground mustard.

SOUTHERN PICKLE SLAW DOGS

MAKES 8 SERVINGS

1/3 cup mayonnaise

2 tablespoons dill or sweet pickle juice

1 1/2 teaspoons balsamic vinegar

1 teaspoon sugar

1/4 teaspoon ground mustard

1/4 teaspoon freshly ground black pepper

1/8 teaspoon salt

1 medium dill pickle, finely chopped (about 2 tablespoons)

1 tablespoon finely chopped onion

1 (16-ounce) bag coleslaw mix

8 all-beef hot dogs

8 hot dog buns

Ketchup and mustard, for serving

In a medium bowl, whisk together mayonnaise, pickle juice, vinegar, sugar, mustard, pepper, and salt until smooth. Add the pickle and onion and stir to combine. Add coleslaw mix and toss with a fork to distribute the dressing. Cover and refrigerate until ready to use.

Preheat a grill to medium-high. Cook hot dogs, turning often, until sizzling and browned all over, 6–8 minutes. Grill the buns, cut side down, until lightly toasted, about 1 minute.

Place a hot dog in each toasted bun and top with some slaw. Serve with ketchup and mustard.

SMOTHERED ITALIAN SAUSAGE GRINDERS

MAKES 4 SERVINGS

1 pound mild or spicy Italian sausage
  (links or bulk)
1 red onion, halved and cut in 1/2-inch slices
1/2 red bell pepper, thinly sliced
4 ounces button mushrooms, sliced

1/2 cup sliced pitted black olives (optional)
1 1/2 cups marinara sauce
4 French rolls
8 slices mozzarella cheese

Preheat oven to 375 degrees F.

If using sausage links, remove casings. Crumble sausage into a large skillet and cook over medium heat, breaking up the meat with a spatula, until browned, about 8 minutes. Drain on paper towels and set aside. Add onion and bell pepper to drippings in the pan and cook over medium-high heat until tender. Add mushrooms and cook until lightly browned, 3–4 minutes. Add olives (if using) and marinara sauce and cook until bubbling, about 5 minutes. Return sausage to the pan and stir to combine. Reduce heat, cover, and keep warm.

Split the rolls lengthwise without cutting through the opposite side. Use your fingers to remove some of the soft bread to make an indentation for the filling. Place 1 cheese slice on bottom half of each roll. Divide sausage mixture evenly among the rolls. Top with another cheese slice and the top half of the rolls.

Wrap each sandwich tightly in aluminum foil. Place on a baking sheet and bake until sandwiches are hot and cheese melts, 12–15 minutes. Serve warm.

GOLDEN SAUSAGE AND CHEESE ROLLS

MAKES 8 SERVINGS

1 pound mild or spicy Italian sausage (links or bulk)

1 medium sweet yellow onion, chopped

3 small cloves garlic, finely minced, divided

$1/4$ cup beef stock

1 teaspoon Worcestershire sauce

1 teaspoon red wine vinegar

1 teaspoon freshly ground black pepper

$1/2$ teaspoon salt

$1/8$ teaspoon onion powder

16 frozen unbaked yeast dough dinner rolls, thawed overnight, at room temperature

1 cup shredded mozzarella cheese

8 tablespoons (1 stick) unsalted butter, melted

$1/4$ cup grated Parmesan cheese

Ketchup and mustard, for serving

If using sausage links, remove casings. Crumble sausage into a large skillet, add onion, and cook over medium heat, breaking up the meat with a spatula, until sausage is browned and onion is tender, 8–10 minutes. Drain any excess grease. Add 2 of the minced garlic cloves and sauté for 1 minute longer.

Add stock, Worcestershire sauce, vinegar, pepper, salt, and onion powder and stir until combined. Cook until mixture bubbles, then reduce heat to medium-low. Cover and cook, stirring occasionally, for 15 minutes. Remove from heat.

(continued)

Grease 2 baking sheets. Gently knead 2 dinner roll dough balls into 1 larger ball; repeat with remaining dough to make 8 large dough balls. Working on a lightly floured work surface, roll each dough ball into a 6-inch circle. Place 1 dough round in a small deep bowl. Spoon 1 1/2 tablespoons mozzarella cheese in the center and top with 1/3 cup of the meat mixture. Bring up sides of dough, pinch to seal, and place, seam side down, on 1 of the prepared baking sheets. Repeat with the remaining dough balls, placing 4 buns on each baking sheet and leaving room between the buns for rising. Cover buns with plastic wrap and let rise in a warm place until puffed, about 30 minutes.

Preheat oven to 350 degrees F.

Combine butter and remaining minced garlic in a small bowl, then brush tops of the buns with some of the mixture. Sprinkle with Parmesan cheese.

Bake until golden brown, 25-30 minutes. Remove from oven and brush with more garlic butter. Cool on a wire rack for 10 minutes. Cut each bun in half with a serrated knife and serve with ketchup and mustard.

SOUPS

CORN AND SAUSAGE BISQUE

MAKES 6 SERVINGS

4 ears fresh corn, husks and silk removed

4 cups chicken stock

1 1/2 cups milk

1 cup heavy cream

1 pound smoked sausage links, cut in
 1/4-inch slices and then halved

1 large onion, diced

1 large carrot, diced

2 stalks celery, finely diced

1 teaspoon salt

1/4 teaspoon freshly ground black pepper

1/8 teaspoon cayenne pepper

1/3 cup crumbled Cotija cheese or grated
 Parmesan cheese

In a large bowl, slice corn kernels from the cobs and scrape each cob into the bowl to release the milk. Break cobs in half and reserve. In a large pot, combine stock, milk, and cream and heat over medium-high heat. Add reserved corn cobs and cook, stirring occasionally, just until mixture begins to bubble. Reduce heat to medium-low and simmer, uncovered, for 30 minutes. Remove from heat, cover, and set aside.

In a Dutch oven or another large pot, cook sausage and onion over medium heat until sausage is lightly browned and onion is translucent, 8–10 minutes. Add carrot and celery and cook, uncovered, stirring occasionally, until tender, about 6 minutes.

Add corn kernels, salt, black pepper, and cayenne. Pour the corn cob mixture through a strainer into the pot (discarding the cobs) and increase heat to medium-high. Bring just to a boil, then reduce heat to medium and simmer, uncovered, until the liquid thickens slightly, about 15 minutes. Ladle into bowls, sprinkle with the cheese, and serve.

SAUSAGE LASAGNA SOUP

MAKES 6 SERVINGS

1 pound sweet or spicy Italian sausage
(links or bulk)

1 large sweet onion (such as Vidalia),
chopped

2 cloves garlic, minced

1/4 cup tomato paste

1 (28-ounce) can whole peeled tomatoes
(preferably San Marzano), chopped and
juices reserved

4 cups chicken or vegetable stock

1 tablespoon chopped fresh oregano or
1 teaspoon dried

1 teaspoon salt

1 teaspoon freshly ground black pepper

4 ounces curly lasagna noodles, broken into
bite-size pieces

1/2 cup shredded mozzarella cheese

1/2 cup grated Parmesan cheese

12 fresh basil leaves, chopped

If using sausage links, remove casings. Crumble sausage into a Dutch oven or large pot, add onion, and cook over medium heat, breaking up the meat with a spatula, until sausage is browned and onion is translucent, 8–10 minutes. Drain any excess grease. Add garlic and cook until fragrant, 1–2 minutes. Add tomato paste and stir until well distributed.

Add the tomatoes with their juices, stock, oregano, salt, and pepper. Bring to a boil, then add the noodles. Cook until noodles are al dente, 12–14 minutes, stirring occasionally.

Sprinkle in the cheeses and stir just until mozzarella starts to melt. Immediately ladle into bowls, sprinkle with basil, and serve.

SMOKED BRATWURST, CABBAGE, AND POTATO CHOWDER

MAKES 8 SERVINGS

2 tablespoons extra virgin olive oil

1 pound smoked bratwurst links, cut in
 1/4-inch slices

2 medium carrots, peeled and cut in
 1/4-inch slices

1 small onion, diced

1 small green cabbage, cut in 1-inch pieces

2 medium leeks, white and pale green parts
 only, cut in 1/4-inch slices

2 stalks celery, diced

2 cloves garlic, minced

6 cups chicken or vegetable stock

1 pound red potatoes, scrubbed and diced

1 bay leaf

Salt and freshly ground black pepper

Heat oil in a Dutch oven or large pot over medium heat. Add bratwurst slices and cook, turning once, until browned, 7–8 minutes. Drain on paper towels and set aside.

Add carrots and onion to the drippings in pot and cook for 5 minutes, stirring occasionally. Add cabbage, leeks, and celery and cook until tender, about 6 minutes. Add garlic and cook until fragrant, 1–2 minutes.

Add stock, potatoes, bay leaf, and browned bratwurst and stir to combine. Bring soup to a boil, then reduce heat to medium-low, cover, and simmer until potatoes are tender, 15–20 minutes. Discard bay leaf. Season with salt and pepper to taste, ladle into bowls, and serve.

SOUP À LA FRANK

MAKES 6 TO 8 SERVINGS

For the croutons

3 tablespoons butter

2 small hot dog buns, cut in 1/2-inch cubes

For the soup

8 cups beef stock

1 pound all-beef hot dogs

2 medium potatoes, peeled and cut in 1/2-inch dice

2 thin carrots, peeled and cut in 1/4-inch slices

1 small sweet yellow onion, diced

1/2 cup diced celery

2 cloves garlic, minced

1 (15-ounce) can tomato sauce

1/2 teaspoon dried thyme

1 (16-ounce) bag coleslaw mix

Salt and freshly ground black pepper

To make the croutons, preheat oven to 350 degrees F.

Melt butter in a large skillet over medium heat. Add bun cubes and toss to coat. Cook, stirring frequently, until just starting to brown, 5–6 minutes. Spread evenly on a baking sheet and bake, stirring once, until crispy, 9–10 minutes. Cool the croutons on baking sheet and set aside.

To make the soup, bring the stock to a boil in a large pot over medium-high heat. Add hot dogs, reduce heat to medium-low, and simmer, uncovered, for 6 minutes. Use tongs to transfer hot dogs to a plate. Tent with aluminum foil and set aside.

Add potatoes, carrots, onion, celery, garlic, tomato sauce, and thyme to the pot and increase heat to medium-high. Bring to a low boil, then reduce heat and simmer until potatoes are fork-tender, 12–15 minutes. Slice hot dogs 1/2 inch thick and add to the pot, along with the coleslaw mix. Cook until cabbage is tender, 6–8 minutes, then season with salt and pepper to taste. Ladle into soup bowls, sprinkle with the croutons, and serve.

EASY-CHEESY KIELBASA-POTATO SOUP

MAKES 6 SERVINGS

2 medium Yukon Gold potatoes, peeled
  and diced
1 pound kielbasa sausage, cut in $1/2$-inch
  slices and then halved
1 medium yellow onion, diced
$4 1/2$ cups chicken stock
$1/2$ teaspoon salt

$1/4$ teaspoon freshly ground black pepper
$1/8$ teaspoon cayenne pepper
1 cup half-and-half
8 ounces sharp cheddar cheese, shredded
Finely chopped fresh flat-leaf parsley,
  for garnish

Put potatoes in a medium pot, cover with 2 inches of cold water, and bring to a boil over medium-high heat. Cook potatoes until just barely tender, about 8 minutes. Drain on paper towels and set aside.

While potatoes are cooking, in a Dutch oven or large pot, cook the sausage and onion over medium heat until sausage is lightly browned and onion is translucent, 8–10 minutes. Using tongs, transfer 6 sausage slices to a paper towel to drain. Finely chop for garnish and set aside.

Drain any excess grease from the pot and add stock, potatoes, salt, black pepper, and cayenne. Bring to a gentle boil over medium heat and cook until potatoes are tender.

Add half-and-half and heat until simmering. Add cheese and cook, stirring constantly, just until cheese melts. Ladle into bowls, garnish with reserved chopped sausage and parsley, and serve.

CHORIZO AND SPANISH RICE SOUP

MAKES 6 SERVINGS

2 tablespoons extra virgin olive oil

1 pound chorizo sausage (links or bulk)

1 medium green bell pepper, seeded and diced

1 medium onion, diced

1 (10-ounce) can diced tomatoes and green chiles, undrained

5 cups beef stock

1 (15-ounce) can tomato sauce

1 (5.6-ounce) package Spanish rice mix

1/3 cup sour cream

1/2 cup shredded Mexican-blend cheese

Heat oil in a large skillet over medium heat. If using sausage links, remove casings. Crumble sausage into skillet and cook for 5 minutes, breaking up the meat with a spatula, then add bell pepper and onion. Cook, stirring occasionally, until onion is translucent and bell pepper is tender, 8–10 minutes.

Add tomatoes and green chiles with their juices, stock, tomato sauce, and Spanish rice mix to the pan. Increase heat to medium-high and bring to a boil. Reduce heat to medium-low, cover, and simmer until rice is tender, 20–25 minutes. Ladle into bowls. Garnish each serving with a dollop of sour cream, stirring once gently with a small spoon to swirl, then sprinkle with the cheese and serve.

SPLIT PEA SOUP WITH CRISPY BROWNED HOT DOGS

MAKES 6 TO 8 SERVINGS

2 cups dried split peas

8 cups chicken or vegetable stock

1 large onion, chopped

2 cloves garlic, minced

Pinch dried thyme

3 stalks celery, chopped

3 carrots, chopped

2 medium red potatoes, diced

6 all-beef hot dogs, cut in $\frac{1}{3}$-inch slices

Salt and freshly ground black pepper

In a Dutch oven or large pot, combine dried peas and stock. Bring to a simmer over medium-high heat. Remove from heat, cover, and let sit for 1 hour.

Bring the soup back to a gentle boil over medium-high heat. Add the onion, garlic, and thyme and cook for 10 minutes. Cover, reduce heat to medium-low, and simmer for $1\frac{1}{2}$ hours, stirring occasionally. Add celery, carrots, and potatoes. Increase the heat to medium and cook, uncovered, until vegetables are tender, about 40 minutes.

Carefully ladle about half the soup into a blender or food processor, working in batches if necessary, and process until smooth. (When blending hot liquids, remove the center cap from the blender lid and hold a kitchen towel over the hole to allow steam to escape.) Return soup to pot, bring to a simmer over medium heat, and keep hot.

Cook hot dogs in a large skillet over medium-high heat until browned on both sides, 8–10 minutes.

Season soup with salt and pepper to taste. Ladle into bowls, top with browned hot dog slices, and serve.

TORTELLINI, VEGETABLE, AND SAUSAGE SOUP

MAKES 8 SERVINGS

1 pound sweet Italian sausage (links or bulk)

1 medium onion, chopped

2 cloves garlic, minced

6 cups beef stock

1/3 cup dry red wine or additional beef stock

4 large tomatoes, peeled, seeded, and chopped

3 thin carrots, peeled and chopped

2 stalks celery, chopped

2 teaspoons chopped fresh basil leaves

1/2 teaspoon dried oregano

1 (8-ounce) can tomato sauce

1 small zucchini, cut in 1/4-inch slices

8 ounces fresh cheese tortellini

1/3 cup grated Parmesan cheese

3 tablespoons chopped fresh flat-leaf parsley

If using sausage links, remove casings. Crumble sausage into a large pot or Dutch oven and cook over medium heat, breaking up the meat with a spatula, until browned, 8–10 minutes. Drain on paper towels and set aside. Pour out all but 1 tablespoon drippings from the pot.

Add onion to the pot and cook over medium heat until translucent. Add garlic and cook just until fragrant, 1–2 minutes. Add stock, wine, tomatoes, carrots, celery, basil, oregano, tomato sauce, and browned sausage. Bring to a boil, then reduce heat and simmer, uncovered, for 30 minutes.

Skim fat from surface of the soup and add zucchini. Cover and simmer for 20 minutes. Add tortellini and cook, stirring occasionally, until tender, 10–14 minutes. Ladle into bowls, sprinkle with Parmesan cheese and parsley, and serve.

SMOKED SAUSAGE AND WHITE BEAN CHILI

MAKES 6 SERVINGS

1 pound spicy smoked sausage links, cut in
  1/2-inch slices and then quartered
1 medium onion, chopped
1 1/2 cups chicken stock
2 (15-ounce) cans great northern beans,
  drained and rinsed

1 (4-ounce) can chopped green chiles,
  undrained
2 teaspoons chili powder
1 teaspoon ground cumin
Salt and freshly ground black pepper
Finely chopped green onions, for garnish

In a large pot, cook sausage and onion over medium heat, stirring occasionally, until sausage is browned and onion is translucent, 8–10 minutes.

Add stock, beans, chiles with their juices, chili powder, and cumin and stir to combine. Increase heat to medium-high and bring to a boil. Reduce heat, cover, and simmer for 15 minutes. Season with salt and pepper to taste. Ladle into bowls, garnish with green onions, and serve.

SALADS AND SIDES

PIZZA PASTA SALAD

MAKES 8 SERVINGS

3 sweet or spicy Italian sausage links

1 pound spiral pasta

3/4 cup extra virgin olive oil

1/2 cup red wine vinegar

1 teaspoon dried oregano

1 teaspoon garlic powder

1 teaspoon pizza seasoning

1/2 teaspoon salt

3/4 cup small grape tomatoes, halved

1/2 cup small fresh mozzarella cheese balls, drained and halved

3 ounces pepper jack cheese, cut in 1/3-inch cubes

1 (2.25-ounce) can sliced black olives, drained

1 small green bell pepper, seeded and diced

1/2 cup shredded Parmesan cheese

Preheat a grill to medium. Cook sausages, turning several times, until cooked through and well browned, 12–14 minutes. Transfer to a cutting board and cut in 1/3-inch slices.

Meanwhile, bring a large pot of water to a boil over medium-high heat and cook pasta according to the package directions; drain and set aside.

In a small jar, combine oil, vinegar, oregano, garlic powder, pizza seasoning, and salt and shake until well combined.

In a large bowl, combine pasta, sausage slices, tomatoes, mozzarella cheese, pepper jack cheese, olives, and bell pepper. Drizzle dressing over salad and stir until well combined. Cover and refrigerate until chilled, about 2 hours. Sprinkle with Parmesan cheese just before serving.

WARM SPINACH SALAD WITH SAUSAGE AND BALSAMIC-MUSTARD DRESSING

MAKES 4 SERVINGS

4 teaspoons extra virgin olive oil, divided

3 (2- to 3-ounce) fully cooked Italian chicken sausage links, cut in 1/4-inch slices

1/2 medium sweet onion (such as Vidalia), cut in 1/4-inch slices

1 1/2 teaspoons balsamic vinegar

1 teaspoon Dijon mustard

4 cups packed baby spinach

Salt and freshly ground black pepper

1/4 cup grated or shaved Parmesan cheese

In a large nonstick skillet, heat 1 teaspoon of the oil over medium-high heat. Add sausage and onion and cook, stirring occasionally, until sausage is lightly browned and onion is crisp-tender, about 10 minutes. Keep warm.

In a large bowl, whisk together vinegar, mustard, and remaining olive oil. Add spinach and toss to coat. Add warm sausage and onion and season with salt and pepper to taste. Sprinkle with Parmesan cheese, toss lightly, and serve.

GERMAN SAUSAGE POTATO SALAD

MAKES 6 TO 8 SERVINGS
■ ■ ■ ■ ■ ■ ■ ■ ■ ■ ■

2 pounds medium red potatoes, scrubbed and halved

8 ounces sliced bacon, roughly chopped

4 fresh German sausage or bratwurst links

2 cloves garlic, minced

1/3 cup apple cider vinegar

3 tablespoons packed brown sugar

1 tablespoon stone-ground mustard

1/2 teaspoon salt

1/4 teaspoon freshly ground black pepper

1/4 cup finely chopped fresh chives

Put potatoes in a large pot and cover with cold water. Bring to a boil over high heat, reduce heat to a simmer, and cook until potatoes are tender, 20–25 minutes. Drain potatoes and cool for 10 minutes. Cut potatoes in 1/2-inch slices and set aside.

Meanwhile, in a large skillet, cook bacon over medium heat, stirring occasionally, until browned and crispy, about 10 minutes. Drain on paper towels. Pour out all but 2 teaspoons of pan drippings and add the sausages to the pan. Cook over medium heat, turning occasionally, until cooked through and browned, 12–15 minutes. Drain on paper towels.

Add garlic to the drippings in the pan and cook over medium heat, stirring, until fragrant, 1–2 minutes. Whisk in vinegar, brown sugar, mustard, salt, and pepper and cook, stirring frequently, until sugar is dissolved and mixture is smooth, about 5 minutes.

Remove pan from heat and add sliced potatoes, gently mixing until potatoes have absorbed all of the liquid. Cut sausage in 1/2-inch slices and gently stir into the mixture. Transfer to a serving dish, sprinkle with chopped chives, and serve warm.

GRILLED ROMAINE AND SAUSAGE CAESAR SALAD

MAKES 4 SERVINGS

2 tablespoons mayonnaise

1 tablespoon fresh lemon juice

1/2 teaspoon Dijon mustard

1/4 teaspoon Worcestershire sauce

1 clove garlic, minced

1/4 teaspoon salt, plus more for seasoning

1/4 teaspoon freshly ground black pepper, plus more for seasoning

1/4 cup extra virgin olive oil

2 (3-ounce) chicken or pork sausage links

2 medium heads romaine lettuce

1/2 cup small grape tomatoes, halved

1/3 cup shaved Parmesan cheese

In a small bowl, whisk together mayonnaise, lemon juice, mustard, Worcestershire sauce, garlic, salt, and pepper until blended. While whisking, add olive oil in a thin stream until thick and well blended. Cover and set aside.

Preheat a grill to medium. Grill sausages, turning several times, until browned and cooked through, about 10 minutes. Transfer to a plate and tent with aluminum foil.

Wash and dry lettuce heads. Trim the root end, leaving most of root intact, and halve lengthwise. Grill the lettuce heads, cut side down, until lightly browned with grill marks, 1–2 minutes. Place 1 lettuce head half on each dinner plate and sprinkle lightly with salt and pepper.

Cut sausages on the diagonal in 1/3-inch slices and arrange over grilled romaine. Drizzle with dressing, sprinkle with tomatoes and Parmesan cheese, and serve.

LOADED CHEESY SAUSAGE POTATOES

MAKES 8 SERVINGS

10 tablespoons butter, melted, divided

1 large sweet onion (such as Vidalia), thinly sliced

8 ounces smoked sausage links, cut in 1/2-inch pieces

1 1/2 cups chicken stock

3/4 cup whole milk

1/2 cup all-purpose flour

1/2 teaspoon garlic powder

1/2 teaspoon salt

1/4 teaspoon freshly ground black pepper

1 1/2 cups sour cream

1 (32-ounce) bag frozen diced hash brown potatoes, partially thawed

2 cups shredded white cheddar cheese, divided

2 cups roughly crushed ridged potato chips

Heat 2 tablespoons of melted butter in a large skillet over medium-low heat. Add onion and cook, stirring occasionally, until soft and well browned, 25–30 minutes. Use a slotted spoon to transfer onion to a bowl and set aside.

Preheat oven to 350 degrees F. Lightly grease a 9 x 13-inch baking pan.

Add sausage to the same skillet, increase heat to medium, and cook, stirring occasionally, until sausage is browned on all sides, 7–8 minutes. Drain on paper towels.

(continued)

In a small saucepan, bring the stock to a boil over medium heat. In a small bowl, whisk together milk, flour, garlic powder, salt, and pepper until smooth. Whisk milk mixture into the stock until fully incorporated and no lumps remain. Reduce heat to medium-low and simmer until bubbling and thickened. Remove from heat and cool for 5 minutes.

Transfer mixture to a large bowl and add sour cream and remaining butter. Add hash browns and sausage and stir together until completely combined. Add 1 1/2 cups of the cheese and onion and stir until well combined. Spread mixture in the prepared baking pan and sprinkle with remaining cheese and the crushed potato chips.

Bake until golden brown and bubbling, about 45 minutes. Cool for 5 minutes before serving.

DEVILED EGGS
WITH SPICY SAUSAGE

MAKES 24 DEVILED EGGS

8 ounces spicy pork sausage (links or bulk)

12 hard-boiled eggs, peeled

1/2 cup mayonnaise

1 teaspoon yellow mustard

1/2 teaspoon curry powder

2 tablespoons diced pimientos, drained

Salt and freshly ground black pepper

Paprika, for garnish

Chopped fresh flat-leaf parsley, for garnish

If using sausage links, remove casings. Crumble sausage into a large skillet and cook over medium-high heat, breaking up the meat with a spatula, until lightly browned. Drain on paper towels, finely crumble, and set aside.

Cut each egg in half lengthwise and gently scoop out yolks into a bowl. Mash yolks with a fork until very smooth, then stir in mayonnaise, mustard, and curry powder until well blended. Stir in crumbled sausage and pimientos. Stir and season with salt and pepper to taste.

Spoon about 1 tablespoon yolk mixture into the hollow of each egg white half. Serve immediately or cover and chill up to 4 hours. Garnish with paprika and chopped parsley just before serving.

ITALIAN GREEN BEANS

1/2 cup slivered almonds

1/4 teaspoon kosher salt

1 1/2 pounds green beans

1 tablespoon extra virgin olive oil

3 sweet or spicy Italian sausage links

1 medium sweet onion (such as Vidalia), sliced

2 cloves garlic, minced

1/2 cup chicken stock

1/2 cup shaved Parmesan cheese

Salt and freshly ground black pepper

Heat a heavy skillet over medium-high heat and add almonds. Cook, without stirring, until barely starting to brown, about 2 minutes. Continue cooking, stirring frequently, until lightly browned and toasted, 2–3 more minutes. Remove from heat, sprinkle with kosher salt, and transfer to a bowl to cool.

Place a steamer basket in a large saucepan. Pour in 1 inch of water and bring to a boil over medium-high heat. Add green beans, cover, and cook until crisp-tender, 5–7 minutes. Drain and set aside.

Heat oil in a large skillet over medium heat. Add sausage links and cook, turning occasionally, until browned and cooked through, about 10 minutes. Drain on paper towels, then cut in 1/4-inch slices.

Add onion and garlic to drippings in the skillet and cook over medium heat, stirring frequently, until onion is golden brown, about 10 minutes. Add green beans, sausage, and stock. Increase heat to medium-high and continue cooking, stirring frequently, until about half the liquid evaporates. Remove from heat. Sprinkle with the almonds and Parmesan cheese, season with salt and pepper to taste, and serve.

SAUSAGE AND APPLE CORNBREAD STUFFING

MAKES 8 SERVINGS

1 (9-inch) square pan prepared cornbread, cut in 1/2-inch cubes

1 (14-ounce) package seasoned bread stuffing mix

1 1/2 pounds pork sausage (links or bulk)

8 ounces sliced bacon, chopped

1 cup chopped celery

1 cup chopped onion

1 pound button mushrooms, sliced

1 cup chopped fresh flat-leaf parsley, plus several sprigs for garnish

2 Granny Smith apples, peeled, cored, and cut in 1/3-inch dice

2 teaspoons dried sage

1/2 teaspoon salt

1/4 teaspoon freshly ground black pepper

3 1/2 cups chicken stock

Preheat oven to 350 degrees F. Lightly grease a 9 x 13-inch baking pan.

Combine cornbread and stuffing mix in a large bowl and set aside.

If using sausage links, remove casings. Crumble sausage into a large skillet and cook over medium-high heat, breaking up the meat with a spatula, until well browned. Drain on paper towels, finely crumble, and set aside.

Pour off the excess grease from the skillet, add bacon, and cook over medium heat until browned. Drain on paper towels. Add cooked sausage and bacon to the cornbread mixture and stir to combine.

Pour off excess fat from the skillet, add celery and onion, and cook over medium heat, stirring occasionally, until transparent and tender, about 5 minutes. Cool for 5 minutes, then stir into the cornbread mixture.

Add mushrooms, parsley, and apples to cornbread mixture and stir to combine. Sprinkle with sage, salt, and pepper and stir until combined. Drizzle with the stock and stir to evenly distribute. Lightly spoon mixture into prepared baking pan without packing down.

Bake until the top is toasted and the center is hot and fully cooked, 40–45 minutes. Cool for 5 minutes, garnish with parsley sprigs, and serve.

SUMMER SWEET CORN SKILLET WITH SAUSAGE AND PEPPERS

MAKES 6 TO 8 SERVINGS

8 ears fresh corn, husks and silk removed

2 tablespoons butter

8 ounces kielbasa sausage, cut in ¼-inch slices and then halved

⅓ cup diced red bell pepper

⅓ cup diced green bell pepper

⅓ cup diced orange or yellow bell pepper

Salt and freshly ground black pepper

Chopped fresh flat-leaf parsley, for garnish (optional)

In a large bowl, slice the corn kernels off the cobs and scrape each cob into the bowl to release the milk; set aside.

Melt the butter in a large, deep skillet over medium-high heat. Add kielbasa and cook, stirring occasionally, until just starting to brown, about 6 minutes. Add bell peppers and cook until tender, 7–8 minutes. Reduce heat to medium, add corn, and cook, stirring occasionally, until tender, 8–10 minutes. Season with salt and pepper to taste and cook for 1 minute more. Sprinkle with parsley, if using, and serve.

CHICAGO DOG SALAD WITH POPPY SEED CROUTONS

MAKES 4 SERVINGS

2 poppy seed hot dog buns, cut in 1/2-inch cubes

3 tablespoons extra virgin olive oil, divided

1 tablespoon butter, melted

1/2 teaspoon garlic powder

1/4 teaspoon salt

1/4 teaspoon ground black pepper

2 tablespoons yellow mustard

2 tablespoons honey

4 all-beef hot dogs

2 cups torn mixed salad greens

1 cup bagged coleslaw mix or shredded cabbage

1/2 cup grape tomatoes, halved

1/4 cup diced dill pickles

1/2 small sweet white onion, quartered and thinly sliced

4 hot banana peppers, chopped

Preheat oven to 375 degrees F.

Put bread cubes on a baking sheet. In a small bowl, whisk together 1 tablespoon of the oil, butter, garlic powder, salt, and pepper. Drizzle mixture over the bread cubes, stirring to coat, then spread

(continued)

them out in a single layer. Bake, stirring once halfway through cooking, until lightly browned, about 15 minutes. Cool on baking sheet and set aside.

In a small bowl, whisk together remaining oil, mustard, and honey; set aside.

Preheat a grill to medium-high. Grill hot dogs, turning several times, until cooked through and well browned, about 8 minutes. Transfer to a cutting board and cut in $1/3$-inch slices.

In a serving bowl, toss together mixed greens and coleslaw mix. Top with warm hot dog slices, tomatoes, pickles, onion, and hot peppers. Drizzle the dressing over the salad and toss gently. Sprinkle croutons on top and serve.

SUPPERS

BRATWURST, HAVARTI, AND CARAMELIZED ONION FLATBREADS

MAKES 2 FLATBREADS (4 TO 6 SERVINGS)

4 tablespoons extra virgin olive oil, divided

1 tablespoon butter

1 large sweet onion (such as Vidalia)

1 teaspoon balsamic vinegar

1 1/2 teaspoons salt, divided

2 cups all-purpose flour, plus more for sprinkling

1/2 teaspoon garlic powder

2/3 cup warm water, plus more if needed

3 smoked bratwurst links, cut in 1/4-inch slices

12 ounces Havarti cheese, shredded and divided

1 teaspoon freshly ground black pepper, divided

1/4 cup grated or shredded Parmesan cheese, divided

Heat 1 tablespoon of the oil and the butter in a large skillet over medium-high heat. Add onion and cook, stirring frequently, until it just starts to turn translucent. Reduce heat to medium-low and continue to cook, stirring every few minutes to prevent sticking, until deep golden brown, 45–60 minutes. Sprinkle with vinegar and 1/2 teaspoon of the salt and stir until combined. Transfer to a heatproof bowl, cover, and set aside.

Add flour, remaining salt, and garlic powder to a food processor and pulse until well mixed. Add water and 2 tablespoons of the oil. Pulse until a dough ball comes together, about 1 minute, scraping

(continued)

down sides of the bowl. (If dough is too stiff, add more water, 1 teaspoon at a time, just until dough comes together.) Transfer dough to a lightly floured surface and knead just until smooth; do not over-knead. Cover the bowl with plastic wrap and refrigerate for 30 minutes.

While the dough is resting, heat remaining oil in a large skillet over medium heat and cook bratwurst slices, turning once, until lightly browned, about 5 minutes on each side. Drain on paper towels and set aside.

Preheat oven to 400 degrees F. Lightly coat a baking sheet with nonstick cooking spray.

Divide the dough in half. On a floured surface, roll 1 ball in a rough oval shape to 1/8-inch thickness. Transfer to the prepared baking sheet, poke the surface all over with a fork, and bake for 10 minutes. Remove from oven and evenly spread with 1/4 of the Havarti cheese and 1/2 of the onion. Arrange 1/2 the bratwurst slices on top and sprinkle with 1/2 of the pepper, 1/4 more of the Havarti cheese, and 1/2 of the Parmesan cheese. Return to oven and bake until the cheeses are melted, 8–10 minutes. Repeat with remaining dough and toppings. Cut into wedges and serve hot.

COMFORTING MOM-STYLE SAUSAGE AND RICE CASSEROLE

MAKES 4 TO 6 SERVINGS
■ ■ ■ ■ ■ ■ ■ ■ ■ ■

1 pound pork sausages (links or bulk)

1 small onion, diced

3 stalks celery, diced

2 cloves garlic, minced

1 3/4 cups chicken stock

1 (14.5-ounce) can cream of celery soup

1 cup long-grain rice

1/4 cup slivered almonds

Chopped fresh flat-leaf parsley, for garnish

Preheat oven to 350 degrees F. Lightly grease a 2-quart casserole dish.

If using sausage links, remove casings. Crumble sausage into a medium skillet and cook over medium-high heat, breaking up the meat with a spatula, until lightly browned. Add onion, celery, and garlic and cook until onion is translucent and celery is tender; set aside.

In a large bowl, whisk together the stock and soup. Add rice and stir to blend. Add sausage mixture and stir until combined. Spread in the prepared casserole dish and top with slivered almonds. Cover tightly with aluminum foil and bake until hot and bubbling, about 50 minutes. Uncover and bake until the top is lightly browned, about 10 more minutes. Cool for 5 minutes, garnish with parsley, and serve.

BEER-GLAZED AND BACON-WRAPPED CHEDDAR-STUFFED BRATS

MAKES 5 SERVINGS

1/4 cup regular or nonalcoholic beer

1/4 cup packed dark brown sugar

10 strips regular-cut bacon

1 teaspoon freshly ground black pepper

5 (4-ounce) fresh bratwurst links

2 ounces mild cheddar cheese

Preheat oven to 400 degrees F. Line a baking sheet with parchment paper.

Combine beer and brown sugar in a small bowl, whisking well to dissolve sugar, and set aside.

Arrange bacon on the prepared baking sheet, overlapping if necessary. Bake for 10 minutes. Reduce oven temperature to 275 degrees F, remove baking sheet from oven, and blot rendered fat from the bacon with a paper towel.

Brush both sides of each bacon strip with the beer syrup. Return to oven and bake for 10 minutes. Remove from oven, brush both sides of each strip with syrup again, and turn the strips over. Bake for 10 minutes. Remove from oven, brush both sides with syrup again, sprinkle with the pepper, and turn the strips over. Bake until lightly browned, about 5 minutes more. Remove from oven and set aside to cool.

Preheat a grill to medium-high. Grill bratwurst, turning frequently, until browned and cooked through, about 12 minutes. Do not turn off grill. Transfer bratwurst to a cutting board and cool for 10 minutes.

Cut each bratwurst lengthwise to within 1/4 inch without cutting all the way through. Cut the cheese in 2-inch-long strips that are 1/4 inch thick, and stuff each bratwurst pocket with cheese. Wrap each bratwurst with 2 strips of candied bacon, securing the ends with toothpicks. Return to grill and cook, turning frequently, until bacon sizzles and cheese starts to melt, 1–2 minutes. Serve warm.

SAUSAGE TATER BOMBS

MAKES 6 SERVINGS

2 pounds russet potatoes, peeled and cut in
  2-inch pieces
9 tablespoons butter, divided
1/2 large sweet onion (such as Vidalia),
  finely chopped

1/3 cup cream cheese, cut in 1-inch cubes
1 cup half-and-half, warmed
1 teaspoon salt
2 cups shredded cheddar cheese, divided
6 (4-ounce) fresh bratwurst links

Put potatoes in a large pot and cover with cold water by 1 inch. Bring to a boil over high heat, reduce heat to a simmer, and cook until potatoes are tender, 20-25 minutes.

While potatoes are cooking, heat 1 tablespoon of the butter in a small skillet over medium-low heat. Add onion and cook, stirring occasionally, until translucent and tender but not browned, 6-8 minutes. Add cream cheese and stir until cream cheese melts. Cover and set aside.

Drain the potatoes well and return to the pot. Cut the remaining butter in 1/2-inch slices and add to potatoes. Lightly mash with a potato masher until the butter is melted and incorporated into the potatoes. Add 7/8 cup of the half-and-half and the salt and mash until incorporated. Add onion and cream cheese mixture and continue mashing. Add up to 2 tablespoons more half-and-half if needed to make a smooth mixture. Cool for 5 minutes, then stir in 1/2 cup of the cheddar cheese; set aside.

Preheat a grill to medium-high. Grill bratwurst, turning frequently, until browned and cooked through, 10-12 minutes. Transfer to a cutting board and cool for 10 minutes.

Preheat oven broiler. Line a baking sheet with aluminum foil. Cut each bratwurst lengthwise to within 1/4 inch without cutting all the way through. Place bratwurst, cut side up, on prepared baking sheet. Pile the mashed potatoes into each bratwurst. Sprinkle remaining cheddar cheese on top. Broil until cheese is melted and lightly toasted, 3-4 minutes, then serve.

CREAMY PESTO TAGLIATELLE WITH SAUSAGE AND MUSHROOMS

MAKES 6 SERVINGS

1 pound Italian sausage links

1 tablespoon extra virgin olive oil

1 pound button mushrooms, sliced

2 cloves garlic, minced

1/2 teaspoon salt

1/4 teaspoon freshly ground black pepper

2 cups heavy whipping cream

1 pound tagliatelle pasta

2 tablespoons prepared pesto sauce

Grated Parmesan cheese, for serving

Chopped fresh flat-leaf parsley, for garnish

Bring a large pot of water to a boil over medium-high heat. Reduce heat, cover, and keep hot.

Meanwhile, in a large skillet, cook sausage over medium heat, turning occasionally, until cooked and browned, about 10 minutes. Drain on paper towels, cool, and cut in 1/4-inch slices; set aside.

Add oil to the same skillet and heat over medium heat. Add mushrooms, garlic, salt, and pepper. Cover pan, and cook, stirring occasionally, for 4 minutes. Uncover and cook, stirring, until the mushrooms are tender and liquid is evaporated, 2–3 minutes more.

Stir in cream and cook, stirring frequently, until mixture bubbles around the edges. Reduce heat to medium-low and cook, uncovered, until slightly thickened, 8–10 minutes. While sauce is cooking, return pot of water to a boil and cook the tagliatelle according to package directions; drain and set aside.

Add pesto to the sauce, stir, and cook just until combined, about 1 minute.

Divide tagliatelle among 6 warmed dinner plates. Arrange sausage on top, pour the sauce over, sprinkle with Parmesan cheese and parsley, and serve.

CORN DOG CASSEROLE

MAKES 6 TO 8 SERVINGS

1 pound all-beef hot dogs, cut in
 1/2-inch slices
1 (8.5-ounce) box corn muffin mix
1 cup sour cream
4 tablespoons butter, melted
1 (14.75-ounce) can creamed corn

1 1/2 cups steamed fresh or frozen corn
 kernels or 1 (15.25-ounce) can whole kernel
 sweet corn, drained
1 (4-ounce) can diced green chiles, drained
1/4 cup finely chopped green onions
1 cup shredded sharp cheddar cheese

Preheat oven to 350 degrees F. Grease a 9 x 13-inch baking pan.

In a large skillet, cook hot dog slices over medium heat until lightly browned on both sides. Remove from heat and set aside.

In a large bowl, stir together muffin mix, sour cream, and butter until combined. Add creamed corn, sweet corn, green chiles, and green onions and stir until well combined Add hot dog slices and stir until evenly distributed. Spread in prepared baking pan and sprinkle with cheese.

Cover with aluminum foil and bake for 50 minutes. Uncover and bake until the top is lightly browned, about 10 more minutes. Cool for 5 minutes and serve.

HIGH-ON-THE-HOG JAMBALAYA

MAKES 6 SERVINGS

4 strips bacon, chopped

8 ounces smoked sausage links, cut in
 1/2-inch pieces

8 ounces all-beef hot dogs, cut in
 1/2-inch slices

1 large onion, chopped

3/4 cup diced green bell pepper

1/2 cup diced celery

1 cup long-grain white rice

1 (14.5-ounce) can whole tomatoes, chopped
 and juices reserved

2 cloves garlic, minced

2 cups chicken stock

1 cup diced cooked ham

1 teaspoon Cajun seasoning

1/4 teaspoon dried thyme

1 bay leaf

Salt and freshly ground black pepper

2 tablespoons chopped fresh
 flat-leaf parsley

In a Dutch oven or large pot, cook bacon over medium heat until lightly browned, about 7 minutes. Stir in sausage and hot dogs and cook, stirring occasionally, for 5 minutes. Add onion, bell pepper, and celery and cook, stirring, until tender, 7–8 minutes. Stir in rice, tomatoes with their juices, garlic, stock, ham, Cajun seasoning, thyme, and bay leaf. Bring to a simmer over medium-high heat, then reduce heat to medium-low, cover, and simmer until the rice is tender, about 30 minutes.

Remove pot from heat, discard bay leaf, and let stand for 5 minutes. Season with salt and pepper to taste, garnish with parsley, and serve.

CHORIZO, AVOCADO, AND BLACK BEAN BURRITO BOWLS

MAKES 6 SERVINGS

2 tablespoons extra virgin olive oil, divided

1 small onion, finely chopped

1/2 medium green bell pepper, finely chopped

1 clove garlic, minced

1 (15-ounce) can black beans, drained and rinsed

1/2 teaspoon salt, plus more for seasoning

1/4 teaspoon ground cumin

1 1/4 pounds chorizo links

1 tablespoon fresh lime juice, divided

1 cup steamed corn kernels, kept warm

Freshly ground black pepper

1 cup cooked white rice, kept warm

4 tablespoons chopped fresh cilantro, divided

1 head romaine lettuce, chopped

2 ripe avocados, peeled, pitted, and cut in 1/2-inch slices

1/2 cup shredded Monterey Jack cheese

1/2 cup pico de gallo or salsa

1/4 cup sour cream

In a large saucepan, heat 1 tablespoon of the oil over medium heat. Add onion, bell pepper, and garlic and cook, stirring, until tender, 6–8 minutes. Add beans, salt, and cumin and cook, stirring, until hot and bubbling, about 5 minutes. Remove from heat and cover to keep warm.

Heat remaining oil in a large skillet over medium heat. Add chorizo and cook, turning occasionally, until browned all over and cooked through, 12–15 minutes. Drain on paper towels, cool, and cut on the diagonal in 1/2-inch slices.

In a small bowl, stir 1/2 tablespoon lime juice into the corn and season with salt and pepper to taste. Sprinkle rice with remaining lime juice and stir in 2 tablespoons cilantro with a fork to evenly distribute.

Divide lettuce among 6 bowls. Divide sausage, beans, corn, rice, and avocado among the bowls and sprinkle with cheese. Top with pico de gallo, sour cream, and remaining cilantro and serve.

SAUSAGE-STUFFED ITALIAN SHELLS

MAKES 6 SERVINGS

1 pound jumbo pasta shells

2 teaspoons extra virgin olive oil

1 pound sweet Italian sausage (links or bulk)

2 cloves garlic, minced

4 cups shredded mozzarella
   cheese, divided

1/2 teaspoon dried oregano

3 cups marinara sauce

1/2 cup grated Parmesan cheese

Chopped fresh basil, for garnish

Preheat oven to 350 degrees F. Lightly coat a 9 x 13-inch baking pan with nonstick cooking spray.

Bring a large pot of lightly salted water to a boil. Cook pasta shells until tender yet firm to the bite, 10–12 minutes. Drain. Lightly brush a baking sheet with the oil. Spread drained pasta shells on the oiled baking sheet to cool.

If using sausage links, remove the casings. Heat a large skillet over medium-high heat, crumble sausage into skillet, and cook, breaking up the meat with a spatula, until lightly browned. Add garlic and cook for 2 more minutes. Remove from heat and drain off excess grease. Cool for 10 minutes, then stir in 2 cups of the mozzarella cheese and the oregano.

Spoon the sausage mixture into the pasta shells, 1–2 tablespoons per shell. Arrange stuffed shells in prepared baking pan. Pour marinara sauce evenly over the stuffed shells. Top with remaining mozzarella cheese. Cover tightly with aluminum foil. Bake until heated through and bubbly, about 30 minutes. Remove foil and sprinkle with Parmesan cheese. Bake, uncovered, until lightly browned, about 10 more minutes. Cool on a wire rack for 10 minutes, garnish with basil, and serve.

FRANKFURTER, POTATO, AND PEPPER SKILLET

MAKES 6 SERVINGS
▪ ▪ ▪ ▪ ▪ ▪ ▪ ▪

1 tablespoon extra virgin olive oil

2 medium russet potatoes, halved lengthwise and cut crosswise in 1/3-inch slices

6 all-beef hot dogs, cut in 1-inch slices

1 small yellow onion, sliced

1/2 red bell pepper, seeded and cut in 1/2-inch pieces

1/2 yellow bell pepper, seeded and cut in 1/2-inch pieces

2 cloves garlic, minced

1/2 teaspoon salt

1/2 teaspoon freshly ground black pepper

Chopped fresh chives, for garnish

In a large skillet, heat the oil over medium heat. Add potatoes and cook, turning occasionally, until browned and almost tender, about 20 minutes.

Add the hot dogs, onion, bell peppers, garlic, salt, and pepper. Cook, stirring occasionally, until hot dogs are lightly browned and peppers, onion, and potatoes are tender, about 15 minutes. Garnish with chives and serve.

FRANKS AND BEANS
WITH APPLES AND BACON

MAKES 4 TO 6 SERVINGS

6 strips bacon, chopped

1 pound all-beef hot dogs, cut in
 1/2-inch slices

1 onion, diced

2 (16-ounce) cans baked beans

1 large Honeycrisp or Granny Smith apple,
 peeled, cored, and cut in 1/4-inch dice

3/4 cup ketchup

1/4 cup yellow mustard

2 tablespoons packed brown sugar

1/2 teaspoon freshly ground black pepper

Preheat oven to 350 degrees F. Lightly grease a 9-inch square baking pan.

In a large skillet, cook bacon over medium heat until crispy. Drain on paper towels and set aside.

Pour out all but 1 tablespoon of the drippings from the skillet and add the hot dogs, cut side down. Cook until lightly browned, flip, and continue cooking until the other side is lightly browned. Use a slotted spoon to transfer hot dogs to the prepared baking pan.

Add onion to the skillet and cook until translucent, about 5 minutes. Transfer to baking pan and add cooked bacon, baked beans, apple, ketchup, mustard, brown sugar, and pepper.

Bake, uncovered, until hot and bubbling, about 45 minutes, and serve warm.

BALSAMIC-GLAZED SAUSAGE, RED PEPPER, AND PEACH SKEWERS

MAKES 4 SERVINGS

1/2 cup balsamic vinegar

3 tablespoons packed brown sugar

2 peaches

1 pound smoked sausage links, cut in
 1/2-inch slices

1 large red bell pepper, seeded and cut in
 1-inch pieces

1 medium sweet onion (such as Vidalia),
 halved and cut in quarters

Salt and freshly ground black pepper

In a small saucepan, whisk together the vinegar and brown sugar. Cook over medium heat, stirring often, until mixture comes to a boil. Reduce heat to medium-low and cook until thickened and reduced by half, 10–15 minutes. Remove from heat and set aside.

To peel peaches, pour enough water into a medium saucepan to cover a peach by 1 inch. Bring to a boil over high heat. Cut a shallow X in the bottom of each peach. Use a spoon to lower 1 peach at a time into the boiling water and blanch for 30 seconds. Remove from water and set aside. When peaches are cool enough to handle, use your fingers to remove the skin. Halve the peaches, remove pits, and cut each half in 4 pieces.

Preheat a grill to medium-high. Thread sausage, red bell pepper, peaches, and onion on skewers. Brush the skewers with balsamic glaze and season with salt and pepper to taste. Grill skewers, turning several times, until the onion is tender and the sausage is lightly charred, 8–10 minutes. Serve hot.

MOZZARELLA-STUFFED SAUSAGE MEATBALLS

MAKES 6 SERVINGS

1 large egg, lightly beaten

1/3 cup Italian seasoned breadcrumbs

1/4 cup grated Parmesan cheese

1/4 cup milk

1/4 cup finely chopped onion

1/4 teaspoon salt

1/4 teaspoon freshly ground black pepper

1 1/4 pounds Italian sausage (links or bulk)

20 mini fresh mozzarella cheese balls

2 cups marinara sauce

Preheat oven to 350 degrees F. Lightly grease a baking sheet.

In a large bowl, mix together the egg, breadcrumbs, Parmesan cheese, milk, onion, salt, and pepper. If using sausage links, remove casings. Crumble sausage into the breadcrumb mixture and mix well.

Shape the mixture into 20 meatballs, pressing 1 ball of mozzarella cheese into the center of each meatball and enclosing it completely. Arrange meatballs on prepared baking sheet. Bake until meatballs are lightly browned and cooked through (160 degrees F), 20–25 minutes. Cool on the baking sheet for 5 minutes, then drain on paper towels.

Heat the marinara sauce in a large skillet over medium heat until simmering. Add cooked meatballs and stir gently. Serve hot.

SAUSAGE STROGANOFF

MAKES 4 SERVINGS

8 ounces uncooked wide egg noodles

2 teaspoons extra virgin olive oil

4 fully cooked chicken or pork sausage links, cut on the diagonal in 1/4-inch slices

1 medium onion, chopped

2 cloves garlic, minced

8 ounces button mushrooms, sliced

1/4 cup all-purpose flour

1/2 teaspoon paprika

1/4 teaspoon salt

1 1/2 cups beef stock

1 cup sour cream

Salt and freshly ground black pepper

Chopped fresh flat-leaf parsley, for garnish

Bring a large pot of water to a boil over medium-high heat and cook noodles according to package directions; drain and keep warm.

Meanwhile, heat oil in a large skillet over medium heat. Add sausage and cook for 2 minutes, then add onion, garlic, and mushrooms. Cook, stirring often, until mushrooms are lightly browned and onion is tender, about 7 minutes.

In a small bowl, whisk together flour, paprika, and salt. Add stock and whisk until combined. Add mixture to the skillet and cook until thickened and bubbling, 3–4 minutes. Remove from heat, add the sour cream, and stir just until combined. Season with salt and pepper to taste. Garnish with parsley and serve over hot noodles.

INDEX

METRIC CONVERSION CHART

VOLUME MEASUREMENTS		WEIGHT MEASUREMENTS		TEMPERATURE CONVERSION	
U.S.	METRIC	U.S.	METRIC	FAHRENHEIT	CELSIUS
1 teaspoon	5 ml	½ ounce	15 g	250	120
1 tablespoon	15 ml	1 ounce	30 g	300	150
¼ cup	60 ml	3 ounces	90 g	325	160
⅓ cup	75 ml	4 ounces	115 g	350	180
½ cup	125 ml	8 ounces	225 g	375	190
⅔ cup	150 ml	12 ounces	350 g	400	200
¾ cup	175 ml	1 pound	450 g	425	220
1 cup	250 ml	2 ¼ pounds	1 kg	450	230